## EXPLORING BIOMES

# FOREST BIOMES

by Lela Nargi

# Ideas for Parents and Teachers

Pogo Books let children practice reading informational text while introducing them to nonfiction features such as headings, labels, sidebars, maps, and diagrams, as well as a table of contents, glossary, and index.

Carefully leveled text with a strong photo match offers early fluent readers the support they need to succeed.

## Before Reading

- "Walk" through the book and point out the various nonfiction features. Ask the student what purpose each feature serves.
- Look at the glossary together. Read and discuss the words.

## Read the Book

- Have the child read the book independently.
- Invite him or her to list questions that arise from reading.

## After Reading

- Discuss the child's questions. Talk about how he or she might find answers to those questions.
- Prompt the child to think more. Ask: There are three kinds of forest biomes: boreal forests, rain forests, and temperate forests. How are they similar? How are they different?

Pogo Books are published by Jump!
5357 Penn Avenue South
Minneapolis, MN 55419
www.jumplibrary.com

Library of Congress Cataloging-in-Publication Data

Names: Nargi, Lela, author.
Title: Forest biomes / by Lela Nargi.
Description: Minneapolis, MN: Jump!, Inc., [2023]
Series: Exploring biomes | Includes index.
Audience: Ages 7–10
Identifiers: LCCN 2021053835 (print)
LCCN 2021053836 (ebook)
ISBN 9781636907536 (hardcover)
ISBN 9781636907543 (paperback)
ISBN 9781636907550 (ebook)
Subjects: LCSH: Forest ecology–Juvenile literature.
Classification: LCC QH541.5.F6 N39 2023 (print)
LCC QH541.5.F6 (ebook)
DDC 577.3–dc23/eng/20211103
LC record available at
https://lccn.loc.gov/2021053835
LC ebook record available at
https://lccn.loc.gov/2021053836

Editor: Eliza Leahy
Designer: Emma Bersie

Photo Credits: Arnain/Shutterstock, cover (left); Mara008/Shutterstock, cover (right); Caleb Foster/Shutterstock, 1; Leigh Prather/Shutterstock, 3; corneliur/Shutterstock, 4; IM_photo/Shutterstock, 5; Pi-Lens/Shutterstock, 6-7; Madlen/Shutterstock, 8; Chodimeafotime/Shutterstock, 9; Leene/Shutterstock, 10-11tl; RECEP_OZTURK/Shutterstock, 10-11tr; Jukka Jantunen/Shutterstock, 10-11bl; jack53/Shutterstock, 10-11br; Milan Zygmunt/Shutterstock, 12-13tl; Erni/Shutterstock, 12-13tr; FotoRequest/Shutterstock, 12-13bl; Anatolii Lyzun/Shutterstock, 12-13br; pstrongerart/Shutterstock, 14-15tl; Aekkarin/Shutterstock, 14-15tr; RAJU SONI/Shutterstock, 14-15bl; Dirk Ercken/Shutterstock, 14-15br; Pulsar Images/Alamy, 16-17; Zhanna Kavaliova/Shutterstock, 18; Evgenii Panov/Shutterstock, 19; lovelyday12/Shutterstock, 20-21; photofriend/Shutterstock, 23.

Printed in the United States of America at Corporate Graphics in North Mankato, Minnesota.

# TABLE OF CONTENTS

**CHAPTER 1**
So Many Trees..................................4

**CHAPTER 2**
Life in Forests.................................8

**CHAPTER 3**
Forests and Us................................18

**ACTIVITIES & TOOLS**
Try This!....................................22
Glossary....................................23
Index......................................24
To Learn More.............................24

# CHAPTER 1

· · · · · · · · · · · · · · · · · · · · · · · · · · · · · · · · · · · ·

# SO MANY TREES

Forest **biomes** cover 33 percent of Earth's land. Forests have many trees. They can be very **dense**. In others, trees grow farther apart.

**redwood tree**

**Temperate forests** get all four seasons.
Redwood trees grow in this forest biome.
They are the tallest kind of tree. They can
grow more than 300 feet (91 meters) tall.
Some are more than 2,000 years old!

**Boreal forests** are in the north. They are cold and snowy. They are also called taigas. The Yukon in Canada is a boreal forest.

**Rain forests** are another kind of forest. Many are near the **equator**. They are warm and wet.

Yukon

# TAKE A LOOK!

Where are Earth's forests? Take a look!

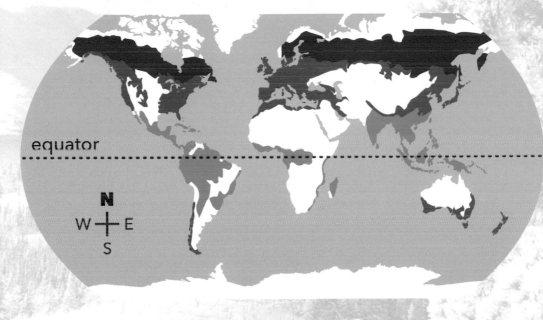

equator

**■ = boreal forest   ■ = rain forest   ■ = temperate forest**

# CHAPTER 2

## LIFE IN FORESTS

Different forests have different kinds of trees, plants, and wildlife. You can find oak, elm, and beech trees in temperate forests. Their leaves change colors in fall. Many drop their leaves before winter.

oak tree leaves

Pines, firs, and spruces are **evergreens**. They keep their needles all year. They grow in temperate and boreal forests.

needles

Temperate forests are full of ferns and mushrooms. Spiders spin webs. Bears and moose roam. Owls hunt mice.

## DID YOU KNOW?

Trees and other forest plants make great food and shelter. About 80 percent of living things call forests home.

lady fern

sheet-web spider

moose

barn owl

pine martin

snow bunting

snowshoe hare

lichen

Boreal forests are home to pine martins and lynx. In spring, snow buntings fly here to raise their young. They fly south for winter. The fur of snowshoe hares turns white in winter. They blend in with snow. Evergreens, lichen, and moss grow.

Kapok, rubber, and banana trees grow in rain forests. They may be hundreds of feet tall to reach sunlight. Vines and orchids also grow. Bright flowers help **pollinators** find them.

Tigers hunt among the trees. Dart frogs' bright colors warn **predators** to stay away.

banana tree

orchid

tiger

dart frog

canopy

A forest has three parts. The top is the canopy. It gets the most sun. Birds and insects rest here. The middle is the understory. It gets less sun. Shrubs and **saplings** grow in this part. The forest floor is shady. Here, you can find moss, ferns, and animals that walk or crawl, such as mice, salamanders, and deer.

# TAKE A LOOK!

What are the three parts of a forest? Take a look!

CANOPY

UNDERSTORY

FOREST FLOOR

# CHAPTER 3

# FORESTS AND US

Forests provide **natural resources**. Trees are made into paper. We build with wood. We also burn it for heat. We eat forest foods, such as fruits and nuts.

wood

We also need forests to fight **climate change**. Cars, homes, and factories give off **carbon dioxide**. This gas heats Earth. Trees turn carbon dioxide into **oxygen** we breathe.

sapling ·····▶

Humans cut down forests to farm, raise **livestock**, and build cities. One way to help is to plant trees. How else can you help forests?

## DID YOU KNOW?

We need forests to help keep our weather just right. Trees in the rain forest release water into the air. This makes more clouds and rain.

# ACTIVITIES & TOOLS

## WATER IN LEAVES

Trees need water to grow. Their leaves release water into the air. Watch how water moves through leaves in this activity!

**What You Need:**

- four small, clear water glasses
- water
- red food coloring
- four green leaves from different kinds of trees, each with about 2 inches (5 centimeters) of stem

❶ Fill each glass halfway with water.

❷ Add enough food coloring to each to make the water dark red.

❸ Place a leaf stem-down in each glass. Only the stems should be submerged in the water.

❹ Observe the leaves for a few days. What happens to them? What does this tell you about how water moves through leaves?

# GLOSSARY

**biomes:** Habitats and everything that lives in them.

**boreal forests:** Forests in the northern parts of the world that are filled with evergreens.

**carbon dioxide:** A gas that is a mixture of carbon and oxygen, with no color or odor.

**climate change:** Changes in Earth's weather and climate over time.

**dense:** Crowded or thick.

**equator:** An imaginary line drawn around the middle of Earth that is an equal distance from the North Pole and South Pole.

**evergreens:** Bushes and trees that have green leaves or needles throughout the year.

**livestock:** Animals that are kept or raised on a farm or ranch.

**natural resources:** Materials produced by the earth that are necessary or useful to people.

**oxygen:** A colorless gas found in the air and water that humans and animals need to breathe.

**pollinators:** Insects or animals that pollinate flowers, allowing them to reproduce.

**predators:** Animals that hunt other animals for food.

**rain forests:** Dense, tropical forests where rain falls much of the year.

**saplings:** Young, thin trees.

**temperate forests:** Forests found in moderate climates.

# INDEX

animals 10, 13, 14, 16, 21
boreal forests 6, 7, 9, 13
canopy 16, 17
carbon dioxide 19
evergreens 9, 13
fall 8
ferns 10, 16
flowers 14
food 10, 18
forest floor 16, 17
leaves 8
moss 13, 16

mushrooms 10
oxygen 19
plants 8, 10
rain forests 6, 7, 14, 21
spring 13
sunlight 14, 16
temperate forests 5, 7, 8, 9, 10
understory 16, 17
weather 21
winter 8, 13
wood 18
Yukon 6

# TO LEARN MORE

**Finding more information is as easy as 1, 2, 3.**

1 Go to www.factsurfer.com

2 Enter "forestbiomes" into the search box.

3 Choose your book to see a list of websites.

FACT SURFER